FATHER

How Your Relationship With Your
Father Affects Your Identity

TJ GILROY

WITH MARY GILROY

Copyright © 2021

TJ GILROY

FATHER FRACTURE
How Your Relationship With Your
Father Affects Your Identity

TJ GILROY
TMG ASSOCIATES PRESS
www.TJGilroy.com

Printed in the United States of America
First Printing 2020
First Edition 2020

ISBN 978-1-7333377-4-8

10 9 8 7 6 5 4 3 2 1

FATHER
FRACTURE

Table of Contents

Introduction 1

Father Fracture 4

This Is Going To Be A Touchy Subject 6

Identity 7

Defining A Father Fracture 10

How A Father Fracture Occurs 14

The Proof 16

Effects Of Fatherlessness 21

My Father As An Example 25

Indicators You Have A Father Fracture 33

Confidence 47

Trust 49

A Final Word On Trust 53

How Do People Perceive The Word *Father*? 55

Healing A Father Fracture 57

The Gift Of Choice 61

Introduction

The concept of fatherhood has been under assault for decades. Although I was aware that many of my friends did not have the same kind of relationship with their dads as I did, it didn't dawn on me that there was a huge problem with the whole concept of fatherhood until my wife and I started counselling people on marriage and other issues at our church. It quickly became apparent that their family foundations were not as solid as my own, and the common denominator was the relationships they had with their fathers. As soon as I asked them to tell me about their fathers, many began to cry because of the deep wounds it revealed. Something was wrong!

There are several issues involved in that assault, namely;

1.   The deliberate attempt to break up what has become known as the nuclear family. Nuclear does not have anything to do with atomic energy in this case, but it refers to a father, mother, and their dependent children as the core, or nucleus, of our society. Several liberal movements say this model of a family is irrelevant and outdated.

2.   The insidious attempt to undermine the role of a father in a family to subvert the role of God as Father. If one's

association with your biological father is bad, then the idea of a loving God as Father is a difficult concept to swallow.

3. The feminization of men to a subordinate role in a family. I heard one pastor refer to this as the "wussification" of manhood. Where fathers were once regarded as the head of a family, they have become something less.

While I believe there is something to be said for each of these issues regarding the problems relating to fathers throughout the world, my focus, and the subject of this book is elsewhere. My take on this subject has to do with the effects your father and the Father (God) have on your identity. Your lack of identity, or false concept of your identity, can often be traced back to your relationship, or lack of relationship, with your father.

As you will see, you receive your identity from your father. If he did a bad job, or no job, then a vital part of who you really are is missing or broken, hence the title Father Fracture. If you have never experienced the unconditional love, approval, security, and provision of a father, then believing that your Father (God) provides those things becomes extremely difficult.

Your identity is much more significant than mere self-realization. If you don't know the real you, you won't be able to find your unique and special GIFT. If you don't discover your GIFT, you will not know your purpose and you will never make the difference for which you were created.

As you read the following pages there are a couple of things that may need clarification. First, "Father Fracture" is capitalized. It refers to the issue of having a fractured relationship with your biological father, and its effects on your relationship with your heavenly Father. Second, whenever "Father" is capitalized, it is in reference to your heavenly Father. When "father" is not capitalized it refers to your biological father.

Mary's Thoughts: My wife, Mary, has provided some comments in specific areas of what follows. A woman's perspective on this critical subject adds value that I could not attempt, and the fact that she had a large Father Fracture of her own adds a great deal of insight to the subject.

Father Fracture

The biggest reason that you may not know the real you is what I call a Father Fracture. As I will explain, you get your identity from your father. This can be a problem.

In your formative years, your father is supposed to be your source of protection, your source of provision, and your source of trust. He is supposed to teach you how to play, how to take risks, and how to empathize with others. He is supposed to love you unconditionally, providing you with confidence in who you are, and giving you real self-worth.

But what if your dad didn't provide you with those things, what if he wasn't there for you, or what if you never knew your father? What if the whole idea of a father makes you feel abandoned, rejected, fearful, or angry? Then from where do you get your confidence?

The fact is that many people have never known unconditional love and approval from a father. They have no idea what they are missing—a real sense of identity, not based on performance, but on who you are. They have a broken concept of a father—a Father Fracture. How can you know unconditional love and acceptance when you have never experienced it? How can you know this vital part of your identity if you don't know it is missing?

It is a critical part of being able to discover the one talent you possess that can be developed to greatness as determined by your very unique way of thinking...your GIFT.

This Is Going To Be A Touchy Subject

A Father Fracture is the number one reason that people don't know who they really are. It is so emotionally and politically charged that I'll bet you won't hear this anywhere else. Many people don't want to reflect on this part of their lives because it opens old wounds. In fact, many people go to great lengths to hide or deny their feelings about their father, so as I discuss these issues, if one or more of them apply to you it may feel as if you are pulling the scab off of a wound. However, if you don't pull that scab off, your wound will never truly heal. It will negatively affect the rest of your life.

For some of you, memories of your father bring back happy times. It reminds you of the love and encouragement you received, and how he helped you in your formative years. But for others of you, those memories are anything but good, or you may have no memories. As soon as someone mentions your father your disposition changes for the worse.

I just ask that as you read through what follows, you don't shoot the messenger. Take some time to see how your feelings about your father affect your thought process and your decisions.

Identity

When someone asks you, "Who are you?" how do you answer? Usually, people will answer by giving their names, but that doesn't really answer the implied question. The implied question is, "How should I know or relate to you?"

As a child, I would answer that I am John Gilroy's son because people knew my father and it was the easiest way to identify me. As I entered adulthood, I would tell people I was a Marine pilot because that described a lot about my persona. But after I left the Marines and someone asked me who I was, it became more difficult to answer. That's because my identity was largely defined by my occupation. (Just an aside —that's why so many people are devastated if they lose their jobs. Too much of who they thought they were was determined by what they did for a living.)

Society has devised some interesting ways to determine who we are, have you noticed? Many people use their Drivers License as identification. It tells your name, your date of birth, your sex, your hair color, your eye color, your height and weight, and your address. In addition, you are assigned a license number by the state so they can look you up in their computer system.

As if that wasn't enough, I recently had to renew my North Carolina driver's license, only to find that I needed additional verification of all these facts if I wanted to use it to pass TSA screening. My new "Real ID" verifies that what is said on the license is actually true. This implies that people lie to authorities about who they are. Could it be that people lie to themselves as well?

In the military, I was issued a military identification card for additional security purposes. If you travel overseas you may need a passport for identification. If you get arrested for some reason you will be fingerprinted for an additional form of identification. In places with very high security requirements they may take a retinal scan or even take a DNA sample in order to definitively identify you.

With all the different ways we have devised to identify you, is that really who you are? Isn't there more to you than fingerprints, height and weight, and DNA? I want to be very clear about what I mean when I say something as provocative as you get your identity from your father.

For the purposes of this discussion, I define your identity as the distinguishing characteristic of your individuality. Your identity contains the values that create your sense of self and determines the choices you make.

> Your identity is the distinguishing character of your individuality.
> It contains the values that create your sense of self and determines the choices you make.

I remember as a child people would tell me things like;

- You look just like your father

- Like father, like son

- You're a chip off the old block

The expectations placed on a child may be that they follow in their parent's footsteps. If your dad was a cop, you'll be a cop. If your mom was a nurse, you'll be a nurse. If your parents owned a business, you would follow on in that business. Even though that frequently happens, it is often at the expense of the person's identity. They become trapped in a role for which they were not created. **This is not what I mean by saying you get your identity from your father.**

Your father shapes your ability to make choices and decisions. He either does this on purpose or by accident. Even if you never knew your father, that fact alone influences your decision-making in ways of which you may not be aware. Your life is the sum of the choices you make, and your ability to choose wisely is greatly influenced by your father.

Defining A Father Fracture

When my wife and I lived in the Chicago suburbs, we attended a large church pastored by Gregory Dickow. He gave several sermons on what he called the Father Fracture. I have not heard anyone else explain this topic, so I give him the credit. A Father Fracture is when you had (or have) a bad relationship (or no relationship) with your father. This will probably lead to having a difficult time having a good relationship (or any relationship, for that matter) with your Father (God).

Pastor Dickow's messages (https://gregorydickow.com/) center on the love that God has for us. He talked about how God loves us the way a father loves his children…and then some. He spoke about the broken hearts many people have because they did not have a biological father that loved them the way God the Father does, and how that can make understanding the love of the Father a difficult concept to grasp. He is also the first person I have ever heard say that a child gets their identity from their father.

Even though his message was not really about how the Father Fracture affects your self-image or your purpose, that is how it appealed to me. His message opened my eyes to the deep hurt that many people feel because of something their fathers either did or failed to do. The effects of their fathers' failures are often devastating and lifelong.

A story from Andrew Wommack's teaching on *The Hardness of Heart* (www.awmi.net) perfectly describes what can happen when someone has a father fracture. This is my paraphrase of the story he told:

"Jane was the youngest of six girls and was six years old when her mother died. Her father was not able to cope with the added responsibilities so he began drinking heavily. Eventually, he put her in an orphanage and promised he would see her every Saturday.

Her first Saturday in the orphanage came and Jane put on her best dress and waited for her dad to come. The other girls in the orphanage asked her what she was doing, and she said, "well, my dad's coming to see me." They laughed and made fun of her and told her that's what they all say and that she would never see him again, he'll never be back.

She argued with the other girls and said, "no way, my dad said he would be back to see me this Saturday!" The other girls were right, he never came back. Every Saturday she would get ready, waiting for her dad to come, but he never came.

Saturday was also the day that they would parade the girls of the orphanage in front of prospective new parents that came to adopt children. The girls that looked like they needed the most help were never picked. Instead, the people always picked the child that seemed the happiest and seemed to have it all together.

Jane learned at a young age, that to get anything, she always had to perform. She would put on a happy face for the prospective parents, looking pretty and portraying that she had it all together.

She grew up in that orphanage, never being chosen by prospective parents, but she did learn how to please people. She became the most popular and the most likely to succeed in her class. She was the head cheerleader and the homecoming queen. She appeared to have it all together on the outside, but it was all a performance. She had learned how to manipulate people, how to look the part, but on the inside, she was still hurting. All of the hurts and all of these fears had never been dealt with.

Finally, she met a man and got married. Jane was still keeping her performance going, getting up every morning at four o'clock to put her makeup on and curl her hair. Her husband never saw her in any other way other than perfectly presented.

Her perfect performance may have lasted longer than some people, but within a month or two after they got married something happened, and they got into an argument. She started crying and her eyes swelled up, her nose got beet red, all of her mascara ran down her face. She looked terrible.

The performance was over now that her husband had seen the real her. Since she was sure he would no longer have anything to do with her, she yelled at him saying, "all right then just divorce me, see if I care."

Her husband looked at her and just laughed. He said, "divorce you because we argued, because we disagree over something?"

Jane's whole life was about trying to gain acceptance from somebody without ever being accepted. She thought that now that her performance was bad, it was over, he was going to divorce her. It blew her away to think that somebody would love her even when she wasn't picture perfect; when she didn't have it all together.

It took her years, but through her husband, Jane began to learn about unconditional love. She learned that somebody could love you even when you weren't worth being loved.

If you were to see Jane today, she is one of the most exciting people to be around. She radiates joy. She has found an acceptance that comes from knowing who she is, and not based on her performance.

Jane had a Father Fracture. The sad fact is that almost everyone has a Father Fracture to some degree, so before dismissing the idea, please allow me to explain the term.

How A Father Fracture Occurs

A Father Fracture can occur for a variety of reasons:

- Your father may have been in the home, but he wasn't really there for you.
- Maybe you never knew your father or he died when you were young.
- He might have deserted your family.
- Maybe your parents divorced, and you felt it was your fault.
- Maybe you had an abusive father.
- He might have made you earn his affection or approval by performing well in school or in sports.
- Maybe nothing you did could ever please him.
- You might have been embarrassed by your father because he didn't live up to your expectations.

No matter the situation, it wasn't good. So, how does that make you feel when someone talks about a "father"? Probably not great.

A Father Fracture is important to recognize in yourself because **you get your identity from your father**. When I say that to people it is like dropping a bomb. That's exactly what

I thought the first time I heard it from Pastor Dickow. Most of us instinctively know how much our identity is influenced by our fathers, but if you had a bad or absent dad it is kind of hard to admit.

Your father is supposed to love you unconditionally, providing you with confidence in who you are, and giving you real self-worth. If you grew up with any kind of a Father Fracture, realizing that you missed these things could be a shock, but it could also explain the hole in your heart that needs to be filled. Most of us have a Father Fracture to some degree, but most of us either don't realize it or don't want to admit it.

Mary's Thoughts: I can still remember where I was sitting in our church the first time I heard Pastor Dickow say that a child gets their identity from their father. I was stunned. As a teenager and into my mid-twenties I had run wild, going from relationship to relationship, sometimes with devastating consequences, and I never really understood why. The instant the pastor spoke those words I had complete clarity about why I had done the things I'd done. The reason was my identity was a mess. I'm not excusing my behavior or its consequences but understanding the "why" of what I had done went a long way to helping me heal.

> You get your identity from your father.

The Proof

I was teaching the idea of finding your purpose to a group of law enforcement leaders a while ago, and all was going well…until I got to the subject of the Father Fracture. The room grew quiet and faces changed. Some looked inquisitive as if I had sparked their interest, while others withdrew. Since these leaders are on the front lines, dealing with the results of Father Fractures that have gone wrong in their communities, many were keenly interested to know more. Others had the wound of their own Father Fracture exposed.

After the training event was over, several of the seasoned cops came up to me privately. They each mentioned that they thought what I said was true, even if it picked a few scabs. What they wanted to know was if I could prove it. Was there evidence or proof that the Father Fracture was real and that one's identity comes from their father? They were interested in the Father Fracture for themselves, but they intuitively understood how this idea had an effect on the communities they dealt with daily.

Well, it turns out there is plenty of evidence, and it is a huge problem that is only getting worse. The challenge is that no one wants to touch this issue with a ten-foot pole.

David Blankenhorn wrote *Fatherless America* in 1995 and since the book was published the issues he described have only gotten worse. He wrote a seminal book about the effects of fathers abandoning their roles in the family and how it is reshaping societies worldwide. He writes, *"Tonight, about 40 percent of American children will go to sleep in homes in which their fathers do not live. Before they reach the age of eighteen, more than half of our nation's children are likely to spend at least a significant portion of their childhoods living apart from their fathers. Never before in this country have so many children been voluntarily abandoned by their fathers."*

He goes on to say, *"The United States will be a nation divided into two groups, separate and unequal. The two groups will work in the same economy, speak the same language, and remember the same national history. But they will live fundamentally divergent lives. One group will receive benefits--psychological, social, economic, educational, and moral--that are denied to the other group.*

The primary fault line dividing the two groups will not be race, religion, class, education, or gender. It will be patrimony. One group will consist of those adults who grew up with the daily presence and provision of fathers. The other group will consist of those who did not. By the early years of the next century (2000) the two groups will be the same size."

One of the things I found remarkable is that until the mid-1800's it was the father, not the mother, that had the primary responsibility for child-rearing, religious and moral education, and societal guidance. It was industrialization that caused the change. Once fathers had to go to work in a factory, as opposed to working on the family farm or business and had to be away from the family all day, these roles shifted to mothers. I point this out because we often assume that the way things are today is how they have always been, but that is simply not true.

The role of mothers has always been one of nurturing. If you look up the etymology of the word *nurture* it means to nourish. The love we receive from our mothers stems from the close and intimate relationship that comes from breastfeeding as a baby, and then from the meals mothers prepare for their families. Only after fathers began working away from the home (as during the industrial revolution) did the primary role of child-rearing shift from fathers to mothers. Believe it or not, it is still within fathers to want to play a significant role in their children's upbringing. But for this to happen, there needs to be a dad at home.

Blankenhorn's book focuses on the cultural effects of fatherlessness, which are enormous. His book does not take into account the role that faith in God has on fatherhood or the Judeo-Christian beliefs of the role of a husband and father. Nor does it does take into account the Judeo-Christian view of adultery and divorce. Nevertheless, he points out that fatherlessness in America is the root cause of:

- Poverty
- Anger
- Promiscuity
- Immorality
- Lack of respect
- Disregard for authority and the law
- Low productivity
- Lack of trust
- Low self-esteem
- Depression
- Loneliness
- Dependence
- Inability to make decisions
- Lack of commitment

Mary's Thoughts: TJ's list of root causes is accurate, although you may not experience all of them in your life. As I looked over the list, I identified several that applied: poverty, anger to some degree (as I liked to argue a lot), promiscuity and immorality, lack of respect, definitely lack of trust, and low self-esteem. The effects of the others were not as noticeable, and I think that is based on my personality.

If you read either of TJ's other books, *Employ Your GIFT, How to Stop Struggling and Live Your Purpose* or *The Purpose Master Key, 7 Steps to Making a Difference by Finding Your Purpose*, he talks about DISC personality profiles.

The DISC profiles help to identity your behavioral tendencies. Your personality profile is very revealing and understanding your natural "wiring" can go a long way toward helping you unlock the real you and heal your Father Fracture.

My only caution is that you need to be honest with yourself when you do the profile. It's about who you think you are, not what others have said you are or should be. My DISC profile helped me take a big step forward in healing my Father Fracture.

Effects Of Fatherlessness

For those of you that like to see the facts, here are some of the issues and statistics found by Blankenhorn. (I have updated the numbers based on the most recent sources available)

- 24% of children lived in father-absent homes in 2019 according to Pew Research.
- Solo motherhood is common among black mothers (56% are in this category). By comparison, 26% of Hispanic moms, 17% of white moms, and 9% of Asian moms are solo parents.
- 50% of all children will live in a single-parent home at some time before they reach age 18.
- In 2019, 41% of US children were born to never-married parents according to the National Center for Health Statistics.
- Half of all children living with a single mother are in poverty, which is five times higher than children living with both parents.
- Children of single parent homes are two times more likely to become obese

Fatherlessness is the leading cause of
poverty in America.

The effects of fatherlessness are devastating. For instance, child abuse is more likely to occur in single-parent homes than when both parents are there. There is also a greater risk of drug abuse, alcohol abuse, mental illness, suicide, and poor educational performance. In women, there is an increase in promiscuity and teenage pregnancy, and in men, there is increased violence and criminality.

I had a dream related to the effects of fatherlessness. In my dream, I saw the word *feckless* as part of the title of a book. The title was on a blue banner with the stars and stripes of the American flag as the background. The sense I had of the dream was that America had become a *feckless* nation.

To be honest, I did not know what the word *feckless* meant, so I had to look it up. A feckless person is weak, ineffective, lacking purpose, and irresponsible. In this sense, irresponsible means a person who is not answerable to a higher authority. All of these traits can be directly attributed to growing up without a father. A person with a good father who loved you unconditionally would not be feckless.

There is a movement by some liberal organizations that says fathers are not necessary for a family except for procreation. This could not be further from the truth. One of the interesting things that David Blankenhorn, author of *Fatherless America,* discovered was the role that fathers have when it comes to playing with their children.

Fathers emphasize play more than the care-taking role that mothers fill. Play is both physically stimulating and exciting. It resembles an apprenticeship or teaching relationship. When fathers play with their children it emphasizes teamwork, competitive testing of abilities, and self-control.

Involved fathers seem to have a special influence on the development of empathy in children. They stress things like competition, challenge, initiative, risk-taking, and independence.

Mothers, on the other hand, are the caretakers. They stress personal safety and emotional security. If you want sympathy or extra attention for some reason, you probably will go to your mom. That is a feature of nurturing, and not normally a strong suit of fathers. If your mom has to fill the role of the father as well as her own role (which is often the case), she is having to do something out of her nature.

Both mothers and fathers are necessary for the development of children. To diminish the role of either fathers or mothers would be a mistake, one that we seem to be making these days. If you didn't receive the unconditional love that your father was supposed to give you, you would have no example by which to recognize the unconditional love your Father (God) has for you.

If the role of the father is assumed by a mother, then her ability to nurture her children is likely diminished from where it would be if a father was also present. Unfortunately, that describes more and more children. They have not benefited from parents the way they could if each were performing their traditional roles in what we call a nuclear family.

Hollywood movies often mirror what is happening in society. Some of my favorite movies are Gladiator, The Kingdom of Heaven, the Star Wars movies, the Star Trek, the DC Comics and the Marvel Comics movies (Batman, Superman, Avengers, Spiderman, Wonder Woman, etc.). All of these have huge Father Fractures as part of their themes. My wife, Mary, likes the romantic "chick flicks," and almost all of them have Father Fractures running through their plots.

It seems that Hollywood has also caught on to the realities of Father Fractures.

My Father As An Example

Many people I speak with today grew up in single-parent families. They consider single-parent families "normal." Even if you were fortunate to have a father in your home when you grew up, was he really there? Did he help you, guide you, and provide leadership in your family? Or did your mom do those things? Even families with two parents often have a dad who is actually absent from the children. Does any of this relate to you?

I have a friend who assumed he had a great relationship with his father. I asked him how often his father hugged him, told him he loved him, or that he was proud of him. He said, "Never, we didn't have that kind of a relationship." That baffled me. What kind of relationship did he think he was supposed to have?

To make matters even more interesting, my friend was also involved in ministry. If his concept of the love of a father was some silent, unspoken man-bond kind of thing (see, I can't relate to that as a loving relationship) then what did he imagine the love of the Father was? Had he never heard God tell him He loved him?

The more I checked into this question, the more I realized **most men and women don't know what a proper**

relationship with their father is supposed to look like. That is mostly because they have never seen one.

> Most people don't know what a proper relationship with their father is supposed to look like.

I asked my wife about this and was surprised by her answer. Her dad died when she was a teenager. Before he passed, he and Mary's mother were separated. There was major tension in their home and a lot of stress due to her dad's alcohol abuse. So, when I asked Mary what she thought a good relationship with a father should look like, she told me she saw it in my father. In fact, she told me how awesome it was for her to see my mother sitting on my father's lap the first time she came over to our home.

Having grown up in a home with a strong and loving father, I took a strong, loving father for granted. My late dad was by no means perfect, but he is still my best example of what a father is supposed to be.

The interesting thing about my dad is that he had a huge Father Fracture of his own. As a teenager, he left home after his tenth-grade year and joined the Marine Corps. The year was 1939, and since the U.S. had not yet entered World War II, he didn't join the Marines out of patriotic fervor. He just wanted to get out of his home situation. Apparently, his father had not gotten along too well with his mother, and his father had a bad habit of spending his paycheck on drinking and "playing the ponies." As the middle of six kids in a rough neighborhood in Philadelphia, and with an alcoholic father and a not so loving mother, Dad needed to escape.

Mom and Dad

By the time I came along, Dad had fought in World War II and Korea. He was the picture of the perfect Marine First Sergeant; he had a booming command voice and all the medals to go with it. If he looked into your eyes, you would swear he could see right into your soul. It was impossible to lie to him.

My earliest memory of my father is the day I thought he was going to kill me. I was four years old, and we lived on Quantico Marine Base in Virginia. Dad was a company first sergeant at the time. The military home we lived in was an old townhouse that had a concrete stoop in front of its front door. Behind our house stood an entire row of similar townhouses, but those had five or six steps that led up to glass storm doors. That row of houses was abandoned, and the entire street was empty—except for me.

I have no idea why, but at four years of age, I had a fascination with breaking glass. I loved to break Coke bottles or light bulbs whenever I got a chance. It was nothing malicious, mind you. I just thought breaking glass was great fun. Well, one day while Dad was at work and Mom wasn't looking, I walked to the abandoned street behind our home. Right in front of me appeared a brick that was perfect for a four-year-old to throw. With great excitement, I walked up the five steps leading to a glass storm door in front of one of those abandoned townhouses, and just as the brick was leaving my hand, a military policeman (also known as an MP) rounded the street corner in his car.

Still oblivious to the MP's presence, but with great joy, I watched the glass door shatter into what seemed like a million pieces. The MP probably watched the whole thing in disbelief. The only thing he asked me before he made me get into the police car, was where I lived. When he knocked at the front door of our home, he had my tiny arm in his big hand, and he had no concern for the tears streaming down my face. I can't imagine what my mother thought.

Mom is German. She had only lived in America for five years at that time, and her English wasn't all that good. She was still new to Marine Corps life on a military base and seeing her son being held by a MP was too much for her. So, Mom called Dad at work and told him to come home because an MP was at the door. She didn't know what to do with me, so she sent me to my room on the second floor. I sat on the edge of my bed with my little legs hanging over, just waiting for my dad to come home. I was sure I would never see my fifth birthday.

Dad walked slowly up the stairs. By that time, I was too scared to cry. He appeared in the doorway, and I looked up at the six-foot, one-inch Marine First Sergeant who was my father. At that time Dad had a forty-six-inch chest and a thirty-inch waist. He was dressed in his khaki uniform; his shirt full of decorations from wars he had fought in.

He looked at me with his best Drill Instructor gaze and asked, "Did you do this?" As I told you, it was impossible to lie to him, so I said "Yes." Then he asked, "Are you sorry?" Of course, I said yes, again. "Are you ever going to do that again?" was his next question, and, of course, I said no. Then the unexpected happened. Dad burst out laughing and had to leave the room because he couldn't stop.

I don't remember what happened after that, probably because the pressure was off. That was the day I learned that there really was a God and that He was merciful because I sure deserved whatever I might have gotten.

This same tough, rugged, highly respected man tucked my sister and me into bed every night. Before we were tucked in, my mom, my sister, my dad, and I would all kneel down by our beds to say prayers. Every night Dad would ask me if I was warm enough, and then he'd kiss me before he left the room. I never once had to guess if I was loved by my parents.

As I grew, Dad was always there for me. I remember, as a teenager, agreeing to take another guy's Sunday morning paper route for him while he went on vacation. At four a.m. on a Sunday morning, I waited on a corner a block away from our house for newspapers to be dropped off. It was dark, I had no flashlight, and rain began to fall. I had no idea what I was doing. I walked home with the papers and sat in the kitchen, crying as I started to wrap the newspapers in plastic.

I didn't want to wake Dad up, because I wanted him to be proud of me, not see me looking like a basket case. Dad must have heard me because he dressed and came downstairs. He never complained about the time or told me how stupid I was; he just helped me deliver the papers. When we were done, he put his arm around me and then went back to bed. Needless to say, I didn't last as a paperboy.

When it came time for me to determine which college to attend and the career I wanted to pursue, my dad let me choose. He let me know it would be great if I went to the Naval Academy to be a Marine Officer, but he didn't insist.

When I told him that I wanted to pursue an ROTC scholarship for the University of Virginia, he said he couldn't be prouder. When I told him that my goal was to become an oceanographer in the Navy, again he was fine with that. Later, when I changed my mind and became a Marine Corps pilot, Dad was ecstatic. But he never imposed his will on me. He did his part by teaching me how to make my own decisions.

Dad was also the unquestioned authority in my life before adulthood. There was no doubt who was in charge and who had the final say in our home. He assumed his role of authority because of his place as husband and father, but he earned our respect because he exercised his authority with strength, stability, and responsibility. Not only was Dad physically stronger than anyone else in the family, but his character and emotional strength were the rock upon which our family's foundation was built. He was stable under pressure, never allowing emotional outbreaks to interfere in his judgment. Dad always took responsibility for whatever anyone in the family did. He took the blame when things went wrong and shared the credit when they went well.

Only after hearing Pastor Dickow speak about the Father Fracture did I realize how truly blessed I was to have grown up with a real father.

No matter what I did, or did not do, my father always told me how proud he was of me and that he loved me. He gave me my identity as an approved son of a great man.

I fully realize that some of you who are reading this had a father as good as mine, or better. But most of you did not. Realizing that you have a Father Fracture is ninety percent of the battle. Until you deal with it, you will not have a firm foundation from which to move forward.

Indicators You Have A Father Fracture

The following are some telltale signs that you have a Father Fracture. (Please note that any one of them could be devastating to you and could leave scars that interfere with knowing your real self. Please also note that these indicators are not in any particular order and I am not making any judgmental statements about your situation.)

- You never knew your father
- Your father abandoned your family
- Your father died when you were young
- Your father was in the home but not there for you
- Your parents divorced
- Your father never, or rarely, told you he loved you
- You felt that you had to earn his approval, affection, or love
- Your father never corrected you
- Your mother did not respect your father
- You had feelings of insecurity as a child
- You were physically or emotionally abused
- You are promiscuous
- You are always angry

- You have gender issues
- You feel offended
- You find it difficult to admit your weaknesses
- You lack confidence
- You find it difficult to trust anyone

You never knew your father

If you never knew your father, you probably discovered early in life that something was missing. Whether it was at a school event, a sporting event, or any other activity that involved a family it was difficult not to notice that other kids had a dad and you didn't. How did that make you feel?

If your father died when you were young you may feel as if something was taken from you. You might blame your father for dying, or you might blame God, you may even blame yourself. Regardless of who gets the blame, you know something is missing.

If your Dad walked away from your family, it is very possible you feel abandoned. Why did he leave? Was it something you did? Didn't he love you? That feeling of abandonment is very hard to shake.

Your father was in the home but not there for you

Maybe you had a father, but he was always too busy for you. Whether it was because he was always at work or had other demands on his time, he was just not there for you. Even when you went out of your way to get his attention, nothing worked. It was as if you weren't important enough for his time. How did that make you feel? How does that make you feel even to this day?

Mary's Thoughts: When I think about the reasons a Father Fracture occurs, several on TJ's list get my attention. Except for the last year of his life, my dad lived in our home, but he wasn't there for my younger sister, my two older brothers, or myself. He rarely ate meals with us. I don't ever recall him attending a school event and when we went to church, he stayed in the back and didn't sit with us. I remember some "family" trips but because of my dad's drinking they were generally pretty tense. I was a freshman in college before I realized that families did fun things with their dad, only because my roommates told me about it.

Your parents divorced

Almost 50 percent of all marriages in the United States will end in divorce or separation; 41% of first marriages, 60% of second marriages, and 73% of third marriages. When those marriages involve children, the children usually end up with the mother. The father is no longer in the home, or at best, infrequently in the home.

Whether parents want to admit it or not, the children in these situations place the blame for the breakup somewhere. Often the children think it is their fault. They cannot imagine their fathers wanting to abandon them, so they must have done something wrong to drive him away. Many of these children carry that guilt with them for the rest of their lives, and that guilt affects their thoughts about marriage, about commitment, and about men.

Your father never, or rarely, told you he loved you

If faith comes by hearing (Romans 10:17), then how does love come? Did you ever have your father tell you he loved you? Did he show it with a kiss or a hug? If not, how do you know he loved you? Even if your love language is not words of affirmation, we all need to hear we are loved. If your father didn't fill that need then who did? Is that void still empty?

Mary's Thoughts: I'm sure my dad loved me but I honestly don't ever remember him telling me. It would have made a huge difference in my life if he had. If you're a parent, I cannot tell you how important it is you tell your children you love them. The verbal expression of your love must be unconditional, not based on performance or behavior and you need to express it frequently.

Being told they're loved gives children the foundation they need to receive the Father's (God's) love. Knowing they're loved by God will be a bulwark in their life against anything the devil uses to try to deceive them. If you've not read Gary Smalley's book, *The 5 Love Languages for Children*, I highly recommend you read it. It will give you great insight on how to express love to each child as they need to receive it.

You felt that you had to earn his approval, affection, or love

If the only time your father approved of you was based on your acceptable performance what happened when you didn't perform? Did he still love you? How do you think this mindset has affected your relationships? Do you demand performance from others before you reward them with love? Is that what you expect from God...that He will only love you if you perform up to His standards?

What if your father had just loved you because you were his child? How might that have changed things? How would that affect the way you loved him? The apostle John tells us that God loves us first (1John 4:10) and that our love for Him is a response. Note that the Father told Jesus He was well pleased in Him BEFORE Jesus had performed any miracles (Matthew 3:17). So, it is clear that we do not have to earn God's love. If anything, He earns our love first.

Mary's Thoughts: To me, approval, affection, or love are different sides of the same coin; either way you're trying to earn something from your father. I relate most to trying to earn my dad's approval. My dad was a well-educated, high-powered local attorney and he had high expectations of me academically. In his words, "if a report card wasn't all 'A's' he didn't want to see it".

Our personalities were very similar, and I was almost desperate for his approval, so my report card was always all "A's". Do you know why? It's because I cheated in elementary school to make sure I didn't fall short of his expectations. If you had to earn affection or approval from your father, have you dealt with the fallout from that habit? The habit of trying to earn approval through performance followed me through college and into my career as a young Naval officer and into my marriage. It will take a conscious effect on your part to break free from performing but you can do it and healing your Father Fracture is worth the effort.

Your father never corrected you

A father that doesn't correct and discipline his children is actually showing that he doesn't care about them. He is abdicating his role in guiding his children and letting them fend for themselves when they have no idea how to do so. This will always end in a lack of respect for your father. Proverbs 13:24 says "the one who loves his child is diligent in disciplining him."

Mary's Thoughts: My dad rarely corrected or disciplined me, and I wish he had. I was a strong-willed child who desperately needed a father's hand to stay on the right track, especially as a teenager. During my early teen years, before my dad died, I was already heading toward promiscuity, yet he never corrected me. He had taught me how to drive a car and shoot a rifle by the age of 10, which was great, but by 14 or so I was drinking and driving. That is terrifying to me today, yet no one ever corrected me.

(A side note: If you're a parent, single or otherwise, I cannot encourage you strongly enough to discipline and correct your children early and consistently. It takes diligence to instill discipline in a child, but the payoff is huge).

Your mother did not respect your father

What possible reasons would a mother have for not respecting her husband? And why would she let that lack of respect be known to her children? If the husband was not fulfilling his role as a provider of security and necessities, if he allowed people to walk all over him, if he violated the trust of the family, or if he abdicated his role of responsibility for the home, then these reasons may be why she does not respect him.

If your mother tells you that your father was not worthy of respect, and that is your image of a father, how much respect do you think you will show other men who are in positions of authority? Then it follows that you will probably not have respect for the Father (God) either.

You had feelings of insecurity as a child

I cannot imagine the feeling of wondering where my next meal was coming from or where I was going to sleep. We never had a lot when we were kids, but my sister and I were secure. In addition to being fed, clothed, and a roof over our heads I always felt physically secure with my dad. I knew my dad would always protect me.

I know that not everyone was so blessed. If you had to worry about any of those things, then your father blew it. That would make trusting God as your provider a very difficult thing because you had to learn to provide for yourself. Surrendering your security to anyone would be very difficult.

Mary's Thoughts: I didn't worry about having enough food to eat or a place to live but I definitely relate to having childhood insecurities. Again, I think different personalities have different emotional responses and that's why it is so important you get to know the real you.

I'm a take-charge kind of personality and my insecurities showed up in feeling an overwhelming sense of responsibility and being very critical of myself. As a kid, I also found it difficult to have fun. I still deal with those things today. If you had an alcoholic or addicted dad as I did, you have a Father Fracture, and healing that fracture is the root of healing your insecurities.

You were physically or emotionally abused

This is another Father Fracture issue I cannot relate to. Your father is supposed to be the one to protect you, not hurt you. If your dad abused you in any way as a child, he did you great harm. As a little girl, it would make it nearly impossible to trust any man, and as a little boy, it sets a terrible example.

Trying to please or get an abusive father to love you can scar someone emotionally and put a real barrier between them and God.

You are promiscuous

Girls that did not receive the appropriate love they were supposed to get from their fathers often look elsewhere to fill the void their fathers created. Since they did not learn what real love from a man was supposed to be like, they often try to get love from men through sex.

A Father Fracture can result in men becoming promiscuous as well. If they did not learn the true nature of love from their fathers, and were not taught to have empathy for people, many promiscuous men will try to lure women into having sex by playing on their need for love. Real love is unconditional but promiscuous men and women have not experienced unconditional love, so they confuse sex for love.

Mary's Thoughts: Promiscuous behavior is rampant in our culture and unfortunately, it's viewed by many as simply the norm. Please don't believe that lie. Promiscuity is defined as having or characterized by many transient sexual relationships or demonstrating or implying an undiscriminating or unselective approach; indiscriminate or casual. That describes my behavior from my teens through my mid-20s. I didn't get my dad's love and attention, so I looked for it in other men determined to fill the hole in my heart.

No matter how casual our society is about sex, promiscuous behavior has deeply scarring consequences: pregnancy, abortion, unwed motherhood, sexually transmitted disease, depression, low self-esteem, and abuse. If a girl doesn't get love and approval from her father, she will, as an old country-western song says, "Look for love in all the wrong places, look for love in too many faces." God, your Father, wants to give you all the love and approval you could ever dream of and He'll do it. Just ask Him to show you how much you're loved.

You are always angry

Where promiscuity is a symptom of a Father Fracture more commonly found in women than men, continuous anger is a symptom of a Father Fracture more found in men than women. Often the men don't know what they are angry about. They just know something is missing, it makes them fearful, which is displayed as anger.

Not all anger is bad, and it is the role of a father to teach sons what is appropriate and what is not. The father's role in teaching empathy shows sons that unrestrained anger can hurt others. Without empathy children only think of themselves.

Mary's Thoughts: I want to share a story with you about anger. For several years I coached a very successful weight loss program and had clients from all across the country, some of whom I never actually met in person. Todd was someone I never met and only coached for a few months. He was obese, weighing over 400 pounds, and was married with two small children.

I remember talking with him on one of our weekly calls and during the discussion, he mentioned that sometimes he'd need to tell his wife to get the kids away from him because he was "getting ready to rage". That got my attention and I felt led to ask him to tell me about his dad. Todd didn't take a half a breath before he said with absolute hatred in his voice "I never knew him". That is a Father Fracture in action. I would also add that obesity often has its root in Father Fracture, and as TJ mentioned above, children of single parents are two times more likely to be obese.

You have gender issues

I know this is a touchy subject, but whenever there is not both a mother and a father in a home the child only has one gender as its example. Most often the single-parent family means that only the mother is there to raise the children, and it is natural for the children to only assume the gender attitudes of the mother.

Mary's Thoughts: I agree gender issues are a very touchy subject, but before you call me a "hater" or throw the book down for what follows, please know I feel compelled to tell you the truth in love. I'm not trying to hurt you or say you are a bad person.

Wrong sexuality presents itself in a variety of different forms and is almost always the result of a Father Fracture. If you fix the fracture, you'll heal your heart and God your Father will help you move away from relationships that are wrong and destructive.

When I was in a wrong relationship, I knew it. I didn't want to admit I knew it, but I did. Cohabitation, homosexuality, lesbianism, bisexuality, etc. are all wrong. People often dull themselves to it, but in the silence of their heart they know. If you're in a wrong relationship, get quiet by yourself and think back over your life looking for rejections, abuses, and disappointments. The relationship is a symptom of the problem, not the root. Father Fracture is the root.

You feel offended

Many people are easily offended. They take everything personally, mainly because they are insecure. The person that offended you often doesn't realize it, and probably did not mean to offend you. Even if they meant to offend you it is still your choice whether you take offense to their comments or not.

Your feelings of offense are often more related to your lack of confidence than in any offensive behavior by someone towards you. When you are secure in your identity it is impossible to take offense. The lack of self-confidence that leads to feelings of offense can be traced to a Father Fracture because you get your identity from your father.

You find it difficult to admit your weaknesses

Not being able to admit your weaknesses comes from having to perform for approval. This could manifest by having to get A's in all your classes, even the ones in which you are weak. It could mean having to excel in all sports, even if you don't like them. Whatever area(s) you were expected to perform well in, you never allowed weakness to show. This kind of expectation can come from both parents, but we are talking about fathers here.

You lack confidence

You find it difficult to trust anyone

The confidence and trust issues that result from a Father Fracture are so important that they deserve their own sections.

Confidence

When you have had the approval of your father, without having had to earn it, you have a source of confidence that lasts a lifetime. When you KNOW you are loved by your father, no matter what you do or don't do, the natural result is to want to please him. You won't need anyone else's approval to make you feel complete.

Having your dad tell you he is proud of you, and that his pride is not coming from your performance, instills a sense of confidence in you that no one can remove. For whatever reason, these things are more important and have a greater effect on you when they come from your father than from your mother. Somehow, mothers are expected to have these feelings and say these things to their children, and it is vitally important to us to have them from our mothers. But if a person doesn't get them from their father, a very important piece of their identity is missing.

Boldness comes from knowing who you are and not fearing the results of your actions. Instead of behaving timidly, as many people who are not sure of themselves do, we should be able to walk boldly, confidently and without fear as someone who is sure they are loved and approved (perfect love casts out fear, 1 John 4:18).

But if you don't know that your Father loves you perfectly, without conditions, and doesn't condemn you (Romans 8:1), then from where do you get your confidence? How could you possibly believe that God chose you (John 15:16), that He gave you a special gift (1Peter 4:10) and that there is a purpose for which you have been called (Romans 8:28)?

On the other hand, what if your Father does love you? Then:

1. You are not condemned
2. You have no fear
3. You are as bold as a lion
4. You have a special gift
5. You are chosen to have results that last
6. You do have a purpose for which you have been called

When you realize that all of this is true, then how confident do you think you will be?

Do you see why the enemy wants you to not know who you really are? The best way to thwart your knowledge of who you really are to your Father is to destroy the concept of a father's love—to create a Father Fracture.

Trust

One of the indicators that you have a Father Fracture is that you have a difficult time trusting anyone. This may not be immediately obvious to you, so let me explain.

When I think of trust, two scriptures come to mind:

1. Luke 18:15-17 (NET)

Now people were even bringing their babies to him for him to touch. But when the disciples saw it, they began to scold those who brought them. But Jesus called for the children, saying, "Let the little children come to me and do not try to stop them, for the kingdom of God belongs to such as these. I tell you the truth, whoever does not receive the kingdom of God like a child will never enter it."

2. Romans 12:2 (NET)

Do not be conformed to this present world, but be transformed by the renewing of your mind, so that you may test and approve what is the will of God—what is good and well-pleasing and perfect.

At first glance, you may not see how these two passages are related, or what they have to do with trust. But they are related, and they have everything to do with trust.

> # The number one thing that God wants from us is to trust Him.

The first passage has to do with how being like a child is crucial to entering the Kingdom of God. But why? Most of us think that being mature, knowledgeable, and wise are the keys necessary to receive all that God has for us. The number one thing that God wants from us, in fact, the only thing that God wants from us, is to trust Him. Trust that what He says is true, and trust that it is better for you than what you hear from anyone else.

Young children, before they are of age to go to school, trust their parents for everything. A real father, as I have already described, provides food, clothing, shelter, security, and love for his children. He is a source of trust for the child, consequently, the child trusts what Daddy says because he or she knows Daddy loves and wants the best for him or her. At this point in the child's life, they have not fallen prey to some other person or entity trying to persuade them that they know better than their daddy. That trust and child-like faith are what God wants from us.

Unfortunately, as we get older, the "world" begins to dissuade us from trusting our father, and our Father. We begin to trust in our teachers, our friends, or government, or even our religion instead of our Father. This is what Paul was warning us about in the second scripture passage (Romans 12:2). He says that we have to be transformed (changed) from the effects of the world. To what? To get back to trusting God. Renewing our mind literally means to get our thinking back to its original condition before it was corrupted by the world…as a child trusts its daddy.

Sadly, many people have never known that kind of trust as a child because they never had a daddy. That is why Jesus referred to the Father as Abba. Abba is a very important word in the Gospel. It is the Aramaic (the language that Jesus probably spoke) word that translates to a more family-oriented word for father; like daddy or papa. It was used by Jesus to let us know that His relationship with the Father was not a formal relationship based on awe or fear, but a relationship of closeness and love. If you have never experienced the trust and love of a father, it makes it more difficult to ever trust God the Father. You will always trust something else before trusting God, or at the least be double-minded. Your Father wants you to trust Him, and the major obstacle to this kind of trust is a Father Fracture.

This lack of trust in your father will spill over into every other aspect of your life. It will result in a small voice in the back of mind telling you not to trust anyone or anything. It will affect your relationships, your marriage, and your purpose. If nothing is trustworthy then your only option is to rely on yourself. You will become self-absorbed, self-centered, and self-seeking. This contributes to depression, suicidal thoughts, greed, and seeking pleasure instead of joy and happiness…and it can happen to the best of us. The remedy…renew your mind. Trust God because He is trustworthy. Your father was supposed to teach you this.

Mary's Thoughts: In our home library we have a copy of an 1828, yes that's very old, Noah Webster dictionary. It defines trust like this: To place confidence in, to rely on, to believe, to credit, to commit to the care of in confidence, to venture confidently. I want you to honestly ask yourself if that's how you feel about your dad and your Father. If you have a Father Fracture it probably isn't.

I've struggled most of my life to trust anybody to do anything. I felt like I could never let my guard down or enjoy myself because of the potential for disappointment. I always feared the loss of a relationship if I didn't meet a goal or someone else's expectations. The only way to break free from the nagging feeling that you'll be let down by someone or you'll disappoint people is to come to the place where you trust your Father and His love for you. His love for you will give you the confidence to be who you really are. It will also assure you that should you blow it or miss the mark His love for you will not change.

A Final Word On Trust

An unforeseen consequence of not being able to trust others is not being able to admit your weaknesses. When you don't trust anyone, the burden is all on your shoulders. You have to do it all and be it all. This could be at home, at work, or even at play. It results in constantly trying to improve your weak points; those areas in which you do not naturally excel. Since you can't trust anyone, you can't rely on anyone to cover your weaknesses, so you have to do it yourself.

That is not fun. When most of what you do seems like a burden, it is difficult to be pleasant with others, it feels like you are constantly under pressure, stress is ever-present, and burnout is inevitable. All of these are the results of not being able to trust others because of a Father Fracture.

Not being able to admit your weaknesses can result in a big problem. If you constantly work to fix the areas that are not strengths, you will find your energy is dissipated and you will feel drained.

Fulfilling your purpose comes from focusing on your GIFT. Your GIFT is the one talent you possess that can be developed to greatness as determined by the unique way in which you think.

You will not be able to develop your God-given GIFT if you spend the majority of your time trying to fix your weaknesses or micromanaging others.

How Do People Perceive The Word *Father*?

Ultimately, a good father has one crucial task. By being a good father—one who loves, approves, protects, provides for, teaches, and guides his children—a father teaches his children about the nature of God. Unfortunately, most of the fathers of today's society have not done a very good job.

For most of society, the word *father* does not bring to mind any of the attributes it should but is often considered a bad word. *Father* often makes people feel neglected, abandoned, or abused. It is no wonder that people are leaving the Church. Who would want to belong to a religion that calls God the *Father* when the word *father* brings up bad feelings and hurt?

> For most of today's society
> *father* is a bad word!

The pastors and ministers who are trying to display and teach the love of God are often unaware of the fact that many of their church members cannot relate to God as Father. In fact, many spiritual leaders have Father Fractures of their own. People can relate to Jesus, or to Christ, or maybe even the

Holy Spirit, but to them, God the Father is a mean, judgmental, and distant being to whom they cannot relate.

That is because their image of a father is as one who abandoned, abused, or berated them. They had to prove themselves worthy of their father's love by their performance.

The idea of a Father (God) that will never leave them or forsake them, and of a Father (God) that does not remember their mistakes does not compute. Since many people have never seen these attributes in an earthly father, it is very difficult to trust that the Father actually loves them. They do not know what they missed by not having a real daddy, and they have no idea why Jesus called the Father "Abba."

To Jesus, His Father was a Daddy. He was someone He could turn to for anything. Jesus even told us we should ask the Father in His name for anything we needed. Since most of us don't see God as our Daddy, we don't really trust Him.

Healing A Father Fracture

Healing a Father Fracture has two parts. The first part is recognizing you have one. You can't fix what you don't know, or won't admit, is broken. If your father did not give you unconditional love, made you work for it, or wasn't there for you, that's not your fault. He did not fulfill his role in helping you form your identity.

He was supposed to play with you, teach to take risks, show you how to be competitive but to play fairly, and enable you to trust. Your dad was supposed to teach you empathy for others and the appropriate respect for authority. His confidence in you was supposed to give you confidence and trust in yourself. This, in turn, would allow you to trust others. If you did not receive these things from your father, you will likely have trust issues for the rest of your life.

If you grew up in a single-parent home (usually meaning no father present) you may have experienced poverty that others just don't understand. It is hard to trust others when you don't know where your next meal is coming from. You may have had to deal with abuse that resulted in your being promiscuous or having a great deal of anger. All of these things may have caused you to doubt yourself, and are the result of not having a father to fulfill the roles you needed.

The second part of healing is finding out for yourself (yes, it is up to you, and no one else can do this for you) that your Father (God) really does love you, approves of you, protects you, provides for you, teaches you, and guides you. He's the one that gave you your personality, your GIFT, and your purpose. He chose these things specifically for you because He wants more for you than you want for yourself.

As Paul says in Romans 2:4, it is the goodness of God that causes people to repent. Repentance doesn't mean crawling uphill over broken glass to prove how sorry you are, as I used to think. To repent simply means to change your mind and change direction. So, changing from being conformed to this world to trusting God comes from a realization that the Father is good and that He really does love you.

Even if you have accepted Jesus as your Lord and Savior you may still have the residual effects of a Father Fracture. That is because your soul (your mind, will, and emotions) still has to be renewed. You may not even be aware that your thinking and emotional responses to everyday life have been affected by your Father Fracture, but they were.

That is why understanding what your Father Fracture is--and we all have one to some degree--enables you to renew your mind in that area. It gives you the knowledge you need to effectively ask God to help you and to reassure you of the love He has for you. Regardless of how mature you are or how small your Father Fracture may be, the depth of God's love for you is so great that understanding it will be a life-long pursuit.

Mary's Thoughts: When I came to the place where I really believed the Father loved me, my life completely changed and so did my relationships with others, including TJ. I stopped fearing what would happen if…and instead I began to trust that God could fix anything I messed up. I'm not telling you to mess your life up but we all make mistakes and you need to trust your Father really knows how to handle any of yours. Believe that and you'll take the pressure off yourself to perform.

If you're wondering how I did it, I'll tell you. First, I got serious about changing my thinking and renewing my mind. I got a Strong's concordance and my Bible and went to work. (A concordance is an alphabetical list of words found in the Bible with their meanings in both Hebrew and Greek along with the passages in which they are found). I studied every definition and passage of trust and fear, and almost every definition and passage of love. I also started listening to pastors and ministers who taught on the love and grace of God. I'm sure there are a lot of good ones but here are some ministries that really helped me: Andrew Wommack (awmi.net); Gregory Dickow (gdm.org), and Creflo Dollar (cdm.org).

Don't worry about learning everything at once, just start. That action alone will help you tremendously and remember that the Father never condemns you and never turns His face away from you. You can come to Him for anything.

The second thing I did was to forgive. Many of you need to forgive others and some of you need to forgive yourself. I couldn't change my past, but I could learn to forgive myself and receive God's forgiveness. If you're thinking it's too hard, or what you did was too bad, or what your dad did to you can't be forgiven, remember forgiving is a choice. Holding unforgiveness in your heart is like drinking poison and thinking the other person is going to die. You can be free from guilt, inferiority, anger, and a host of other negative emotions by choosing to forgive.

The Gift Of Choice

Even if your father blew it, and I'm sure he did in some way, your Father doesn't. He loves you so much that he wanted you to be born. He gave His Son for you so that you could have a loving relationship with Him, and He gave you His Spirit to help you every step of the way.

But the greatest gift that God gave you, besides the gift of life, is your unique ability to think. I say unique, because no one thinks in exactly the same manner as you. Without the ability to think, none of us would be able to make choices, we would not be able to make decisions, and we would have no control over our futures. We get to choose to accept the love and gifts that God gives us.

A Father Fracture can influence the choices you make because of its potential to distort your thinking. Your real identity allows you to make the best choices for your life, but if you think you have to perform to earn love, or you never really know yourself because your dad messed it up for you, then your decisions may not be as good as they should be.

A short story from Mark Twain describes why your choice is so important. It goes like this:

A man died and met Saint Peter at the Pearly Gates.

He said, "Saint Peter, I have been interested in military history for many years. Who was the greatest general of all time?"

Saint Peter quickly responded, "Oh that's a simple question. It's that man right over there."

"You must be mistaken," responded the man, now very perplexed. "I knew that man on earth, and he was just a common laborer."

"That's right my friend," assured Saint Peter. "He would have been the greatest general of all time, if he had been a general."

The would-be general missed it. He missed the purpose for which he had been created. Far too many people go an entire lifetime with their GIFT still undiscovered, and the biggest reason for that is their Father Fracture.

Without knowing you have a Father Fracture and how to deal with it, it is virtually impossible to know your real identity. If you don't know the real you, you will not be able to know your purpose. Making a difference in life then becomes a crap shoot…it will all be based on luck.

Your Father doesn't operate based on luck. He says,

"I know the plans I have for you, plans to prosper you, not to harm you. I have plans to give you a future filled with hope."
Jeremiah 29:11 NET

My hope is that you will choose to recognize and heal your Father Fracture and enjoy God's plan for you; one of hope and prosperity.

To learn more, visit www.TJGilroy.com

TJ GILROY

Are you struggling?

Do you feel like something is missing but you don't know what?

It could be that you:

- don't like what you do for a career.
- feel like everything is a struggle.
- lack confidence.
- don't know your value.
- are drifting through life.

All of these are symptoms of the same issue:

you don't know your Special GIFT.

In *Employ Your GIFT* you will discover that:

- You have a **Special GIFT**; everyone does.
- It is special because **only you** have your GIFT.
- Employing your GIFT is your **purpose**.
- Operating in your GIFT is what **makes a difference**.

You can choose to continue to struggle or you can choose to Employ Your GIFT.

TJ Gilroy

Author of *Employ Your GIFT,*
How to Stop Struggling and Live Your Purpose

Available at www.TJGilroy.com

Made in the USA
Middletown, DE
07 November 2023

41949358R00045